Ruth Thomson

Chrysalis Children's Books

First published in the UK in 2002 by
Chrysalis Children's Books
An imprint of Chrysalis Books Group Plc
The Chrysalis Building, Bramley Road, London W10 6SP

Paperback edition first published in 2004

ISBN 1 84138 259 0 (hb)
ISBN 1 84138 851 3 (pb)

British Library Cataloguing in Publication Data
for this book is available from the British Library.

**Editors**: Mary-Jane Wilkins, Russell McLean
**Designers**: Rachel Hamdi, Holly Mann
**Illustrators**: Patrice Aggs, Becky Blake, Louise Comfort,
  Serena Feneziani, Charlotte Hard, Brenda Haw, Jan McAfferty,
  Kevin McAleenan, Holly Mann, Melanie Mansfield, Colin Payne,
  Lisa Smith, Sara Walker, Gwyneth Williamson
**Educational consultant**: Pie Corbett, Poet and Consultant
  to the National Literacy Strategy

Printed in Hong Kong
10 9 8 7 6 5 4 3 2 1 (hb)
10 9 8 7 6 5 4 3 2 1 (pb)

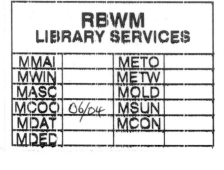

# CONTENTS

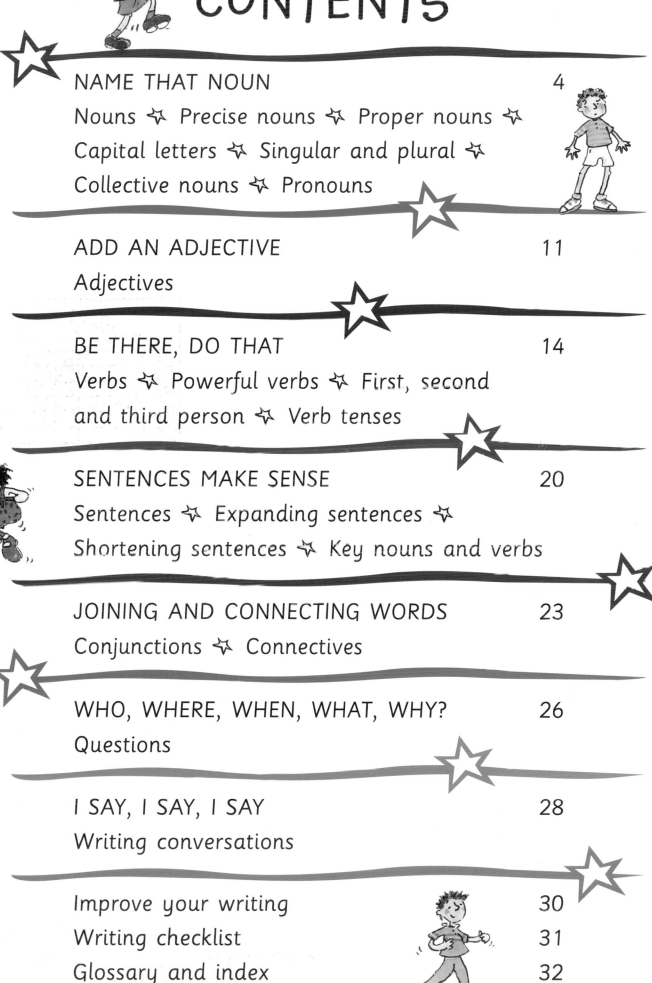

## What is a noun?

A noun is a naming word for:

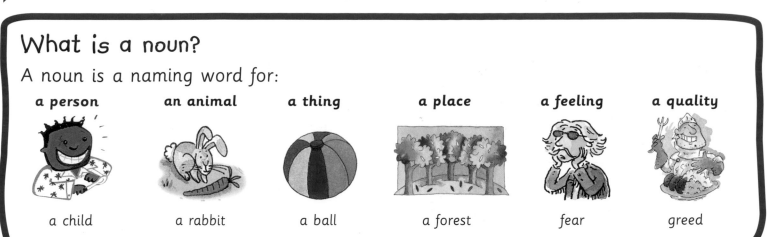

| **a person** | **an animal** | **a thing** | **a place** | **a feeling** | **a quality** |
| a child | a rabbit | a ball | a forest | fear | greed |

## That reminds me

Choose a **person**, then a **thing**, then a **place**, in turn, that reminds you of the previous word, like this.

A **mermaid** (person) reminds me of a **mirror** (thing).

That reminds me of a **pond** (place).

That reminds me of a **fisherman** (person).

That reminds me of **fish and chips** (thing).

That reminds me of the **seaside** (place).

And so on...

## Add the labels

All these nouns label parts of this space machine. Use them to help you label a space machine of your own.

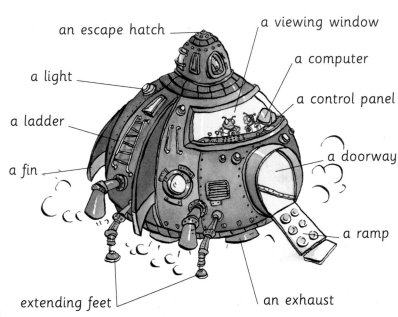

an escape hatch

a viewing window

a computer

a light

a control panel

a ladder

a doorway

a fin

a ramp

extending feet

an exhaust

Draw an elephant. Write labels for the parts of its body.

## Whizz bang!

The fairy waved her wand and look what happened.

The **ball** changed into an **elephant**.

The **farmer** changed into a **hen**.

## THINGS TO REMEMBER

To discover if a word is a noun:

- Put **a**, **an**, **the** or **some** in front of it. Does it make sense?
- Does it tell you the name of something?
- Can you add another word to tell you more about it?

Write some more sentences like these, changing one noun into another. Make them as silly or as funny as you can.

---

## Pack a punch!

Look at the nouns in this sentence.

The **man** and the **woman** rode by **horse** to the **town**.

When the nouns are more precise, the sentence becomes more interesting.

**Sir Boastalot** and **Sophia** rode on **Bess** to **London**.

Rewrite this sentence, making the nouns more precise.

The **man** and the **boy** tied up the **girl** and crept out of the **house**.

## Writing tip

★ Use precise nouns to make your writing more powerful.

## Hunt for nouns

 Make a list of all the nouns in this piece of writing.

The explorers put up their tents near a pool. A crocodile watched them with beady eyes. Cook unpacked his rucksack and checked his equipment.

First he found the bottles, the spoons, the forks, the cooking pot and the rolling pin. Next, he counted the bowls, the glasses and the mugs. He spotted the jug, the jar and the kettle.

But where was the cooker?

## Making a list

Jane has unpacked her rucksack.

 Make a list of the things she needs for the night. Make another list of the things she will need for her trip into the jungle.

## Writing tips

When you write a list:

☆ Use commas to separate the items,
eg the *bottle*, the *spoon*, the *fork*

☆ Do not put a comma *before* the word **and**,
eg the *bowls*, the *glasses* and the *mugs*

## What is a proper noun?

Nouns that describe the names of particular people, buildings, towns, countries, rivers, seas, days of the week, months and festivals always start with a capital letter. They are called proper nouns.

Mei    Joe

Ferndale Forest

Frampton Castle

New York

## Hunt for capital letters

Find all the capital letters in this piece of writing. Which are names? Which ones are the first letter of a new sentence? Which are both?

On Monday, 30 April, the Jolly Roger set sail across the Atlantic Ocean for Treasure Island. The captain was Mrs McFee. Big Joe was in charge of the stores, Ruthless Rosa was the navigator, Little Louis was the lookout and Minnie Minor played jigs on her accordion to keep everyone happy.

On Tuesday, 1 May, Captain McFee spied land.

"Perhaps it's Treasure Island!" exclaimed Big Joe.

"It can't be," yawned Little Louis. "We haven't sailed far enough yet!"

 Where do you think the pirates have reached? Write about what they did on Wednesday, 2 May.

**7**

# What are singular and plural nouns?

★ Nouns can be **singular** (just one) or **plural** (more than one). You can turn most singular nouns into plurals by adding **-s** or **-es**.

**tomato**
**tomatoes**

**toothbrush**
**toothbrushes**

**car**
**cars**

★ These are some exceptions. Keep a list of any others that you find.

**foot**
**feet**

**mouse**
**mice**

**child**
**children**

★ **Collective nouns** describe a group of things.

An **army** of ants

A **bundle** of sticks

A **flock** of sheep

A **bunch** of flowers

A **plate** of peas

## Hunt for plurals

List all the plural and collective nouns in the sentences below.

The family sat by the river to eat their picnic. Suddenly, a cloud of gnats whined over their heads. Two ducks waddled by, followed by a gaggle of honking geese. Next, a party of ramblers clomped past in muddy boots.

✏ Who might come by next? Continue the story. Include both plural and collective nouns.

## What are they called?

Invent collective nouns for these things.

balls     bottles

streamers     fishermen

skyscrapers     kites

### Writing tip

When you use nouns in the plural, you may need to change the spelling of the verb.

The dog **barks**. ➡ The dogs **bark**.

## Singular or plural?

Draw two columns and label them **Singular** and **Plural**. List the nouns from the writing below in the right columns.

*The prince and his army travelled from beyond the mountains, over the hills and through deep forests to visit the king. With his sword in one hand and his shield in the other, the prince galloped towards the drawbridge.*

*Inside the castle, the cooks were preparing a feast. One was roasting a pig. Another stirred a cauldron of stew. The impatient king and queen paced the battlements, while the bored princess gazed out from her bedroom window.*

Look at the picture and see how many other nouns you can add to your lists. Write what happened next, using your lists to help you.

## Quick change

Make these singular nouns plural. Write two lists – plurals which end in **-s** and plurals which end in **-es**. Which are the odd ones out?

bush     man     tree
church     princess     village
dog     sheep
field
house

## What is a pronoun?

A pronoun stands in place of a noun.

The boat has a leak. **It** begins to sink.
Mr Fox is worried. **He** calls for help.

### Useful pronouns

| | | | | |
|---|---|---|---|---|
| I | you | he | she | it |
| we | they | me | us | them |
| my | your | his | her | their |

The bees buzz around Mr Fox.
**They** annoy **him**.

---

## Say a sentence!

Take turns to say a sentence, beginning with a different pronoun each time.

**I** have freckles.

**You** have curly hair.

**They** are best friends.

**She** likes apples.

### ☀THINGS TO REMEMBER

- Some pronouns are male or female.
  Jim yelled. **He** yelled again.
  Jane fell over. **She** hurt her knee.

- Pronouns can be singular or plural.
  They agree with the noun they replace.
  Mum opens the door. **She** opens **it**.
  The boys swap cards. **They** swap **them**.

---

## Find the pronouns

Make two columns, headed **Noun** and **Pronoun**. Read the sentences below. Write any nouns you find in the first column. Write the pronouns connected to the nouns in the second column.

One day, the children made a snowman. They gave him a carrot nose. Then they had a snowball fight. Jill threw a snowball at Bob. It hit him in the eye and he fell over. Pete made a pile of snowballs and threw them at Anya. She ran away to escape them.

| Noun | Pronoun |
|---|---|
| snowman | him |

# ADD AN ADJECTIVE

## What is an adjective?

An adjective tells you more about a noun, such as:

| its size | its shape | its colour | its feel | its character | its weight |
|---|---|---|---|---|---|
|  |  |  |  |  |  |
| a **small** chick | a **rectangular** tray | a **golden** key | a **soft** blanket | a **fierce** crab | a **heavy** hamper |

## Adjectives galore

You can use all the adjectives below to describe this troll.

| | | |
|---|---|---|
| stinking | enormous | fierce |
| big-eared | hungry | sneaky |
| stupid | hairy | drooling |

eg An **enormous**, **sneaky** troll

or

The troll looks **hungry**.

Can you think of any more?

## Describe it

How many adjectives can you think of to describe these animals? Think about their colour, size, smell, sound and the feel of their coats.

a fox

a parrot

a wild boar

### THINGS TO REMEMBER

To discover whether a word is an adjective:

- Can you put it in front of a noun?
  eg the **angry** man
- Can you put it after verbs such as
  **is, are, feels, looks, gets** or **seems**?
  eg the man looks **angry**
- Does it tell you more about a noun?

## Hunt for adjectives

 Write down the adjectives in the sentences below.

The exhausted explorers reached a cliff.

"Let's take a short cut across that wooden bridge," suggested Cookie.

"It looks dangerous," shivered Skipper.

She leant over the steep side and spotted a narrow path leading down to the winding river.

"I hope the stepping stones aren't slippery," she murmured. "That crocodile looks very hungry."

## Too many adjectives!

 The writing below has too many adjectives. Write your own version. Choose the best adjectives or make some of the nouns more precise.

Mr Magill and Jane decided to cross the old, shaky bridge. As they reached the other, far side, it broke. The others took the long, winding, rocky way down to the flowing, shallow water.

Nimble, agile Skipper leapt across the smooth, flat, steady stones. But as Scout crossed the river, the lazy, ferocious, green crocodile snapped his jagged, sharp, white teeth.

Now describe what happened next.

## Writing tips

✫ Don't use too many adjectives. Choose unusual ones.

✫ Don't use two adjectives that mean the same thing. Every adjective should add new information about a noun.

✫ Sometimes you can use a more precise noun instead of an adjective.

✫ If you use more than two adjectives, separate them with a comma.
eg The **green, slinky** snake

## Writing instructions

Instructions do not need many adjectives. You only need them to make it clear exactly what to do. Find the adjectives in these instructions for making tomato sauce.

1. Chop two onions into small pieces.

2. Fry them in oil until they are golden.

3. Add three teaspoons of tomato purée.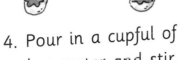

4. Pour in a cupful of hot water and stir.

5. Simmer until the sauce is thick.

## Adding adjectives

 Rewrite these instructions, adding some adjectives to make them clear. Use the pictures to help you.

1. Cut apples into slices. Put them into a pan.

2. Add tablespoons of sugar.

3. Mix in tablespoon of raisins.

4. Heat the mixture until it is...

5. Stir in tablespoons of yoyhurt.

## Exactly the opposite!

Do the adjectives in the sentences below fit the picture? List each adjective on a separate line. Beside each one, write its **opposite**, using the picture to help you. Write a new version of the text using these opposites.

The cross bride opened her tiny window to get a breath of stale air on the dull, rainy morning.

Just then, the scruffy bridegroom came past, carrying a round tray. It was loaded with a plate of soggy toast, raspberry jam and a cup of cold coffee.

"Horrible morning," he called out.

Suddenly, the calm bridesmaid fell off the new bridge into the muddy water below.

# BE THERE, DO THAT

## What is a verb?

A verb is the word that tells you what is happening in a sentence.

He **rows** ashore.  She **likes** this book.  The jungle **is** dense.  She **feels** excited.

## Guess what I'm doing!

Take turns to mime an action. See who can be the first to guess what you are doing.

Are you **singing**?

Are you **diving**?

## Change the meaning

Try each of these verbs to make a sentence. See how the meaning of the sentence changes.

**sees**

**climbs**

**finds**

**gazes at**

**reaches**

**trudges up**

The man **dreams about** the mountain.

## Think of a verb

Think of new verbs for the sentences below. Write as many different verbs as you can.

The cat **squeezes** the rat.

The girl **walks** to the town.

The boy **throws** the ball.

## Using powerful verbs

Here is one way of changing verbs to make them more powerful. Write your own version of these sentences, choosing different powerful verbs.

Clare and Ahmed ~~went~~ **journeyed** into the dark forest. They ~~went~~ **stumbled** along a narrow path, ~~cutting~~ **slashing** the undergrowth as they ~~went~~ **advanced**. They were ~~looking~~ **searching** for rare animals. They ~~looked~~ **peered** in every direction, but they did not ~~see~~ **glimpse** a single one.

## Writing tips

✰ Every sentence needs a verb.
✰ You can use verbs in chains, eg **was eating**; **have been walking**
✰ Choose powerful verbs to give your writing impact.
✰ Choose precise verbs to say exactly what you mean.
✰ Use a thesaurus to help you choose verbs.

## Disaster!

Imagine you are one of the characters in the scene below. Use powerful verbs to write about a disaster that strikes the island. Include what you can hear, smell and feel, as well as what you can see.

## First, second and third person

Different types of text are written in a particular person.

★ In the first person, the writer talks about himself or herself, using the pronouns **I**, **we**, **my** and **our**.

   eg **I** met **my** friend.

★ In the second person, the writer talks to you. Sentences begin with a verb, with "you" left out.

   eg **Fold** the paper in half.
   **Cut** along the fold.

★ In the third person, the writer tells what happened to other people, using the pronouns **he**, **she**, **it**, **they**, **his**, **her** and **their**.

   eg **They** found a ring. **It** was very shiny.

## What person is this?

Read these sentences. Who is the writer talking about? What person is she or he writing in? Continue one piece of writing in the same person.

**Get off** the bus at Grange Road. **Walk** towards the hospital. **Turn** right at the traffic lights into Russell Street. **Cross** the road and **walk** as far as the garage.

**Abdul** stared at **himself** in the mirror and made **his** wish. Slowly, very slowly, the mirror began to tilt sideways and **Abdul's** reflection began to fade.

Yesterday, **I** stayed in the camp all day writing **my** diary. **We** hope it will stop snowing soon, otherwise **we** will never reach the Pole. **Our** food supplies are getting low and so are **my** spirits.

### THINGS TO REMEMBER

- Letters, diaries and some narratives are written in the **first** person.
- Instructions, rules and directions are written in the **second** person.
- Recounts and narratives are often written in the **third** person.

## Instructions

If aliens landed on Earth, they would need all sorts of instructions about living here.

**How to wash up dirty plates**
1. Fill a sink with warm water.
2. Add a squirt of washing-up liquid.
3. Swish the water until it foams.
4. Scrape bits of food off the plates.
5. Brush the plates in the soapy water.
6. Rinse them under the tap.
7. Put them in a plate rack to dry.

## How to do it

 Write some instructions about one of these topics.

How to ride a scooter or bike

 How to make a sandwich

How to clean a fish tank

 **Writing tips**

When you write instructions:

☆ Start each sentence with a verb, eg **Fill** a sink with warm water.

☆ Only use adjectives if you need them to explain what to do, eg **soapy** water

## Changing person

Do you know the story of Goldilocks? She went into the house of the Three Bears, while they were out for a walk. She broke Baby Bear's chair, ate all his porridge and fell asleep on his bed. When the Three Bears came home, they frightened her so much that she ran away.

 Rewrite the story in different ways.

★ Write a page of Goldilocks's diary, using the **first** person. It might start like this:

Yesterday, **I** did a very daring thing. **I** went...

★ Write a cross letter from Baby Bear to Goldilocks, using the second person. It might start like this:

Dear Goldilocks,
   **You** are really...

★ Continue the story in the third person, like this:

When **Goldilocks** reached home, **she**...

## What is a verb tense?

The tense of a verb tells you when something happened.

★ The **present** tense describes events that are happening now, such as:

Sheep **eat** grass.

★ The **past** tense describes events that have already happened, such as:

She **picked** some flowers.

## Instructions

The verbs in instructions are always in the present tense. Find the verbs in this magic spell.

### AN INVISIBILITY SPELL

Crush some dried maggots. Mix them with a handful of chopped nettles. Boil the mixture in vampire blood. Leave to cool. Sprinkle with toenail clippings.

Drink this potion on the last stroke of midnight. Turn around three times and stamp twice to become invisible.

 Invent your own magic spell, using some of the verbs below.

| | | |
|---|---|---|
| slice | roll | melt |
| smear | fill | fry |
| add | beat | dip |
| whisk | mix | split |
| stir | rub | put |
| tap | tie | bake |

## Reports

Reports are also written in the present tense.

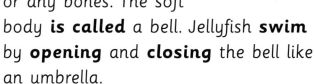

Jellyfish **live** in the sea. They **have** soft bodies and long tentacles, but they **do** not **have** a brain or any bones. The soft body **is called** a bell. Jellyfish **swim** by **opening** and **closing** the bell like an umbrella.

Jellyfish **use** their tentacles to **sting** fish and other prey. The most deadly jellyfish **lives** in Australia. Its powerful sting **can kill** a person within minutes.

 Write a report about an animal that you like.

 Writing tips

✰ Write reports, instructions and explanations in the present tense.

✰ When you finish writing, check that you have not changed tenses anywhere.

## Writing in the past tense

Narratives and recounts are usually written in the past tense.

★ Many verbs in the past tense end in -**ed**, such as play**ed**, liv**ed**, look**ed**, happen**ed**.

★ Some verbs change in the past.

They **go**. ➡ They **went**.

I **see**. ➡ I **saw**.

He **runs**. ➡ He **ran**.

## All change

Can you say the past tense of these verbs?

| | | |
|---|---|---|
| take | find | sleep |
| stand | come | is |
| have | feel | |
| hold | catch | |

## Sentence sorting

Are these sentences in the **past** tense or the **present**? Which is an instruction, a report, an explanation or a recount?

On 24 August 79 AD, the volcano erupted. Stones and ash showered the city of Pompeii.

 Tadpoles breathe through gills and eat with horny teeth and lips.

Cut the pineapple and oranges into chunks. Mix them with grapes and cherries.

 Every autumn, swallows migrate to warmer places where they can find plenty of insects to eat.

 Write some sentences of your own, one for each type of writing.

## Present to past

 This writing has slipped from past to present tense.

Friday the thirteenth was an unlucky day for Ali. It all started when he missed the bus for school. As he waits for the next one, it begins raining. By the time the bus finally arrives, Ali is soaked. Miserably, he slumps into a seat and hunts in his rucksack for his purse.

Rewrite it all in the **past** tense. Then continue the story, making sure you stay in the past tense.

# SENTENCES MAKE SENSE

## What is a sentence?

Sentences have an **actor** (a subject) and an **action** (a verb).

★ A sentence always starts with a capital letter and ends with a full stop. A sentence makes sense.

**The hungry lion**

★ This is not a sentence. It is not complete. It has an actor, but it doesn't have an action.

**The hungry lion roared**.

★ This is a complete sentence. It has an actor and an action.

## Make a sentence

Write some funny sentences, using these actors (subjects) and actions (verbs).

For example:
The menacing alien fell into the garden pond.

**Actors**

The happy king

The busy robot

Merlin, the magician

The brave princess

The forgetful elephant

The genie of the lamp

**Actions**

... lost the magic key.

... scared away the monsters.

... was frightened by the loud thunder.

... yelled loudly.

... tripped over the fallen tree trunk.

... fought the fiery dragon.

... danced all night.

... gave me a present.

## As short as possible

Take turns to think of a complete sentence that is as short as possible.

**Jewels sparkle.**

**Jen waves.**

**The cat purred.**

## Expanding sentences

You can make a short sentence longer by adding extra information.

The man pointed.

The **old** man pointed **at the moon**.

The old man **in a green suit** pointed **excitedly** at the **full** moon.

The old man in a green suit pointed excitedly at the full moon **hanging heavily in the sky**.

## Longer sentences

 Expand these three sentences. Use the pictures to help you.

The fox snarled.

The boy gasped.          The man drove.

## Journey into the unKnown

 Expand these sentences to write a story about going to an unknown planet.

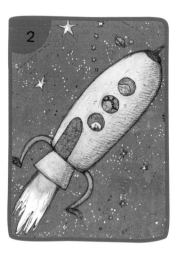          

The rocket blasted off.          The rocket zoomed.

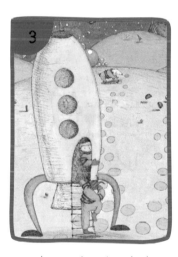          

The rocket landed.          The astronauts explored.

## Writing tips

⭐ Start all sentences with a capital letter. Put a full stop at the end.

⭐ Make sure every sentence has an actor (subject) and an action (verb) to make it complete.

⭐ Make your sentences interesting by using precise nouns, exciting adjectives and powerful verbs.

# What are connectives?

Certain words and phrases connect sentences together, to tell the reader the order of events. These are called time connectives.

**First**, Jim swam across a lake.

**Then** he climbed a mountain.

**Later on**, he skied back down again.

**After that**, he lifted his weights.

**Next**, he made some soup for supper.

**When** he finished eating, Jim fed his animals.

**Before** he went to bed, he planned the next day's route.

**Finally**, Jim lay in his tent and gazed at the stars.

## PLAY THE GAME  Jim's day

Take turns to describe what Jim did the next day, using a time connective to start your sentence.

**After** breakfast, Jim brushed his teeth.

**Meanwhile**, his hungry dog gnawed a bone.

**When** he had packed his tent, Jim set off.

## Writing tips

☆ Time connectives are especially useful for writing instructions and stories.

☆ You can put these time connectives at the beginning of a sentence or as a link between two sentences.

| | |
|---|---|
| first | suddenly |
| then | after a while |
| next | later |
| after that | meanwhile |
| next day | later on |
| finally | all of a sudden |
| just then | last of all |
| when | early |

# What next?

 Write your own version of this sentence. Replace every **and then** with a more interesting connective. Break the text into several sentences.

*I was rowing across the lake **and then** the boat started rocking wildly **and then** there was a loud splash **and then** I heard a low roaring **and then** I turned round **and then** I saw a huge creature looming above me **and then** it opened its huge mouth **and then** I dived into the water to escape.*

# Tell the story

 Describe the events of this story, using connectives to tell the reader what happened **first**, **next** and **last**.

# WHO, WHERE, WHEN, WHAT, WHY?

## What are questions?

Questions are sentences that ask for something. They end with a question mark (?).

★ Questions that ask for information often begin with question words, like these.

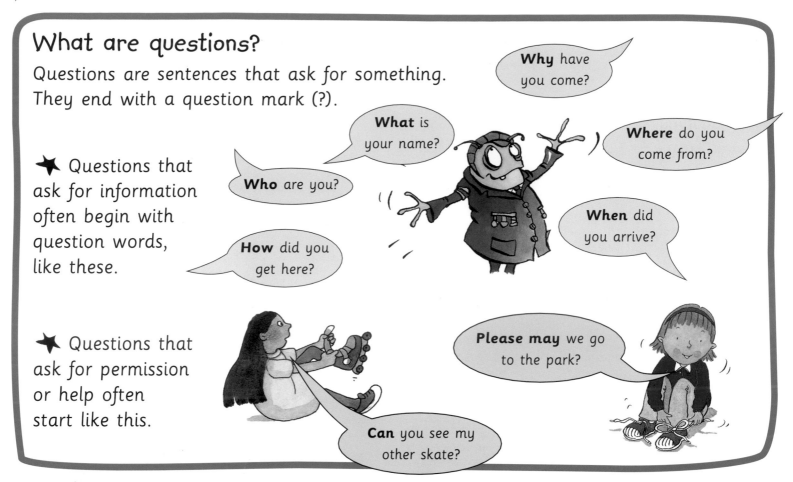

**Why** have you come?

**What** is your name?

**Who** are you?

**Where** do you come from?

**When** did you arrive?

**How** did you get here?

★ Questions that ask for permission or help often start like this.

**Please may** we go to the park?

**Can** you see my other skate?

## What's the question?

Which questions would prompt these answers?

**Gemma** scrubbed the dog.

Gemma scrubbed the dog **in an old tin bath**.

Gemma scrubbed the dog **because he was muddy**.

Gemma scrubbed the **dog from next door**.

Gemma scrubbed the dog **after its walk**.

Gemma scrubbed the dog **hard**.

## Planning a recount

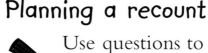 Use questions to help you plan a recount. Write some questions for one of these sentences, using the question words: Who? What? Where? Why? When? How?

Then write a short recount, answering your questions.

Paul rang the bell.

Mr Morrow shouted.

The animal escaped from the cage.

## Asking questions

 Write some questions you might like to ask one of these characters. Invent some interesting or funny answers.

**Q** Your majesty, why do you wear a glittering crown?

**A** It hides my bald spot.

A dragon

A mermaid

A fortune teller

## A list of questions

When you are planning to write about a topic, you often need to do some research first. You could make a list of questions about the information you want to know, using the question words: Who? Where? When? Why? What? How?

To find out about the invention of aeroplanes, you might ask some of the questions in the panel opposite.

 Write a list of questions for one of these topics.

 planets

whales

 lightning

volcanoes

 submarines

knights

**Who** built the first aeroplane?

**When** was it built?

**What** was it made of?

**Where** did it take off?

**How** far did it fly?

# I SAY, I SAY, I SAY

## Writing conversations

Conversations are set out in a particular way to make it easy for readers to follow.

★ Each different speaker starts on a new line.

★ The first word someone says starts with a capital letter.

★ The words that someone says are enclosed inside speech marks.

★ Powerful verbs describe how these people speak. These are shown in **bold** type.

★ A comma, a full stop, a question mark or an exclamation mark shows the end of what someone says. It is inside the speech marks.

"Mum, Dad, Sam!" **yelled** Tara at the top of her voice. "Come and see this!"

"Stop shouting so loudly," **snapped** Mum, as she got out of the car. "You'll disturb the neighbours."

"What's the big fuss?" **enquired** Dad.

"Let's go and see," replied Sam, impatiently.

"Hurry up, you slowcoaches," **shouted** Tara excitedly.

The family gathered by the front door and stared in amazement.

"Who can have given us this?" asked Mum, frowning.

 What have the family found? Continue their conversation.

## Just imagine

Write an imaginary conversation between two very different characters, such as:

a kind princess

and

an evil queen

a lazy lion

and

a sneaky fox

# Storytime

In a cartoon strip, the words people speak are put in speech bubbles.

Rewrite the story, changing the speech bubbles to speech, using speech marks.

## What did you say?

Take turns to think of something to say. Choose a verb (instead of said) to describe how you might say it, such as, "I whispered." Say your sentence out loud in the way your verb describes.

# Improve your writing

★ Read this first draft of a piece of writing.

Once upon a time Kay went to the park and she saw a robbers stealed a handbag and then she ran after him and they ran past the swings past the roundabout and on towards the pond and the duck all fly up in the air.

"Stop. said Kay. "Why should I" said the robber. And at that moment along came a policeman. He got the robber by the arm and handcuffed him.

★ Check for errors and see whether you can improve the writing.

One day
~~Once upon a time~~ Kay ~~went to~~ the park ~~and~~ was playing in when

she saw a robber**s** steal~~ed~~ a handbag**.** ^and

Quick as a flash
~~then~~ she ran after him and ~~they ran~~ past the chased him

swings^, past the roundabout and on towards

the pond^. ~~and~~ the duck^s ~~all~~ fl**ew** up in the air. T s

!" shouted ? replied
"Stop~~.~~ ~~said~~ Kay. "Why should I"^ ~~said~~ the

Just
robber. ~~And~~ at that moment ~~along came~~ a appeared on the scene
policeman^. He ~~got~~ the robber by the arm grabbed
and handcuffed him.

★ Write out your final draft with all the corrections.

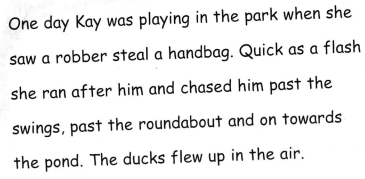

One day Kay was playing in the park when she saw a robber steal a handbag. Quick as a flash she ran after him and chased him past the swings, past the roundabout and on towards the pond. The ducks flew up in the air.

"Stop!" shouted Kay.

"Why should I?" replied the robber.

Just at that moment a policeman appeared on the scene. He grabbed the robber by the arm and handcuffed him.

# Writing checklist

When you have finished your first draft, read it through carefully.
Check the following points before you write the final draft.

## ★ Sentences

- Does every sentence have a verb?
- Are the sentences different lengths?
- Do the sentences start in different ways?
- In conversations, does each new speaker start on a separate line?

**SENTENCES MAKE SENSE**

## ★ Verbs

- Are the verbs in the same tense throughout the draft?
- Are the verbs powerful?
- Do the verbs agree with the nouns?

## ★ Nouns

- Do the names of people, places, days, months and festivals start with capital letters?
- Have you changed some nouns to pronouns, so they are not repeated too often?
- Have you made the nouns precise?

## ★ Adjectives

- Does every adjective add new information about a noun?
- Can you sometimes use a precise noun instead of an adjective?

## ★ Punctuation

- Does the first word of every sentence have a capital letter?
- Does every sentence end with a full stop, a question mark or an exclamation mark?
- Are there commas between the words in a list?
- Is there a comma between two adjectives?
- Are the words that people speak inside speech marks?

**NOUNS ARE NAMES**

# Glossary and index

An adjective adds to a noun. It tells you more about somebody or something.

> The **stupid** troll ate the **mouldy** bread.

A comma is a punctuation mark inside a sentence. It tells the reader when to pause. Commas separate things in a list or any extra information in a sentence.

> Angie put on her coat**,** her hat**,**
> a scarf and a pair of gloves.

A connective is a linking word in the middle of a sentence or between two sentences.

> **First**, Jim swam across a lake.
> **Then** he climbed a mountain.

Conversations report what someone says in the speaker's own words.

> **"Look at that plane,"** shouted Jamal.

An exclamation shows a strong feeling or gives an order. It ends with an exclamation mark (**!**).

> **"Get out!"** screamed Susie.

A noun names a person, a thing, a place, a quality or a feeling.

> a **boy**, a **horse**, a **forest**,
> **excitement**

A **collective noun** refers to a group.

> a **pack** of dogs

A **proper noun** names a particular person, place, day of the week, month, festival or organization. It starts with a capital letter.

> **New York**, **Friday**, **August**, the **Red Cross**

A pronoun takes the place of a noun.

> The boat has a leak. **It** begins to sink.

A question is a sentence that asks something. It ends with a question mark (**?**).

> **Who built the first aeroplane?**

A sentence describes an event or a situation. It has an actor (subject) and an action (verb) and makes sense. It starts with a capital letter and ends with a full stop, a question mark or an exclamation mark.

> **The hungry lion roared.**

Speech marks show the beginning and end of direct speech.

> **"What's the big fuss?"** enquired Dad.

A verb is the word that describes what is happening in a sentence.

> She **laughs**. The dogs **bark**.

The verb tense tells you when something happens – either now (in the present) or in the past.

> He watch**es**. (present)
> He watch**ed**. (past)